MW01246008

BELLS.

Evening Chimes.

T. H. ROLLINSON.

How Can I Leave Thee.

OLD GERMAN

Blue Bells Of Scotland.

Alice, Where Art Thou?

ASCHER.

Oliver Ditson Company
April 1, 1910

GT. 26a.

The Palms.

FAURE.

Love's Old Sweet Song.

J. L. MOLLOY.

4

I Am The Merry Postilion

F. ABT.

Allegretto.

My Sweetheart

Allegro moderato.

KJERULF.

Cherry Ripe.
MAZURKA.

BELLS.

T. H. ROLLINSON.

Love's Golden Dream.

LENNOX.

Softly Gliding Polka.

T. H. ROLLINSON.

The "Home Stretch."
GALOP.

BELLS.

J. H. RAYDER.

Two Marionettes.

EDITH COOKE

67851-78-Bells

Milton Keynes UK
Ingram Content Group UK Ltd.
UKHW021549280724
1054UKWH00012B/156